SIX STRATEGIES
FOR WAR

ASIAPAC COMIC SERIES
STRATEGY & LEADERSHIP

The Practice of Effective Leadership

SIX STRATEGIES FOR WAR

六 韜

WANG XUANMING

Translated by
Alan Chong

ASIAPAC . SINGAPORE

Publisher
ASIAPAC BOOKS PTE LTD
629 Aljunied Road
#04-06 Cititech Industrial Building
Singapore 1438
Tel: 7453868
Fax: 7453822

First published July 1993
Reprinted December 1993

© ASIAPAC BOOKS, 1993
ISBN 9971-985-99-3

Cover design by Bay Song Lin
Typeset by Quaser Technology Private Limited
Body text in 8/9 pt Helvetica
Printed in Singapore by Loi Printing Pte Ltd

Publisher's Note

Comics play an important role in our fast-moving urban society. They serve the young as well as the adult readers. Comics are fun and entertaining. They can also be a kind of satire and can even make classical literature and philosophy available to us in a light-hearted way.

We are pleased to present the work of Wang Xuanming, a contemporary cartoonist from Mainland China, who has illustrated a series of ancient Chinese military classics into comics. *Thirty-six Stratagems*, the first book in this series, has been warmly received by our readers. *Six Strategies for War*, the second book in the series, is produced to meet the keen demand for Chinese military classics.

We feel honoured to have the cartoonist Wang Xuanming's permission to the translation rights to his best-selling comics. We would also like to thank Mr Alan Chong for translating this volume and writing the Foreword, and the production team for putting in their best effort in the publication of this series.

Armchair strategizing is a luxury for us who live in peace. Our nation is fortunate to be able to live in peace and prosperity at a time when a myriad conflicts are taking place around the world. But heed the words of King Baudouin of the Belgians: "It takes twenty years or more of peace to make a man; it takes only twenty seconds of war to destroy him."

Armchair strategizing is no idle pastime. It is precisely the thing to do in peacetime if one is to be prepared for a war which may yet come. As is said so succinctly in Chinese, " 居安思危 ". However, our preparations would be in vain without some form of strategies.

The strategies described in *Liu Tao* have been proven by the successes of those who knew them, and the blood of those who did not, as the many illustrations from Chinese history show.

The publication of this comic version of *Liu Tao* is warmly welcomed, as is the earlier publication of *Thirty-six Stratagems*, its companion book in the series. These two books do much to make ancient wisdom accessible, even to the young. Their translation into English will reach an even wider audience. While the weapons of war have changed, it is still men who must fight wars. Understanding the ways of men goes a long way towards understanding the ways of war.

In this regard, *Liu Tao* is much more than a book of strategies in warfare. The Civil Strategy is very much applicable to human resource management. Yao's handing over of his throne to Shun, a commoner, is an example of good leadership, as is Zhao Jianzi's sacrifice of a favourite white mule for the sake of a subordinate. Similarly, the Dragon Strategy while subtitled "The Wisdom of Military Leadership", is applicable to leadership in general. The example of General Wu Qi of Wei who rewarded his men based on their merit and not on their rank is not an easy one to follow. Indeed, high-ranking officers are often awarded medals without any great feat on their part. In his autobiography "Memoirs of an Infantry Officer", war poet Siegfried Sassoon tells of an officer being awarded a medal for teaching bayonet fighting while never having been near any fighting.

This rendition of *Liu Tao* has been thoroughly enjoyable. I await the publication of the three remaining books in the series and the lessons they have to offer.

Chiang Ming Yu
Chairman, Wargame Club
Singapore Armed Forces Reservist's Association

About the Editor/Illustrator

Wang Xuanming, a contemporary cartoonist in China, was born in Beijing in 1950. He was trained formally in commercial art and industrial art. Since 1972, he has been engaged in various aspects of artistic work, even undertaking the production of screen advertisements and artistic stage designs. Wang's contribution to the field of art is immense. He frequently explores various ways of expressing his artistic talents. Besides a lot of cartoons, picture books, and illustrations, he also does oil paintings and posters. His works have on many occasions entered nationwide art exhibitions, won awards in several art competitions, and have been selected for inclusion in various art albums.

Wang's cartoons, illustrations, and other works have been serialized in all the major newspapers and publications in Beijing since 1980. His cartoons entitled *Different Gravitational Force* is praised by famous Chinese artists, and was selected for inclusion in the *Anthology of Chinese Scientific Cartoons*. In 1987, he participated in the creation of the animated cartoon *Brother Elephant*, which captured the hearts of many children when it was first shown on television.

Wang has worked with many publishers in Beijing, such as China Friendly Publishing Co., Chinese Cultural Publishing Co., Huaxia Publishing Co., People's Art Publishing Co., and Zhaohua Publishing Co. He has gained the trust and confidence of both publishers and artists alike.

In his latest comic series, *Books of Strategy*, he uses a simple and humorous art form to introduce ancient Chinese military classics to modern readers. The books were very well received by people from all walks of life when they were first published in China; the Beijing Radio Station made a special interview of this series of books and highly recommended it to the public. This series is published by China Friendly Publishing Co. in China, and by Treasure Creation Co. Ltd. in Hongkong. Asiapac Books in Singapore is the publisher for the English edition of this series.

Wang is at present an art editor at the *China Science and Technology Daily*.

Foreword

Military books are an important part of ancient Chinese literature. Indeed, among some 600 titles listed in an early Eastern Han (AD 25-220) catalogue, about 10 per cent were military books.

Many of them have been lost. Among those that survive today, the most famous is a collection of seven books known as *Wu Jing Qi Shu (The Seven Books of War)*. The leading classic of this collection is the world-renowned Sun Zi's *Art of War*. A less famous member of the collection, but highly regarded by rulers and generals of ancient China, is *Liu Tao*, or *Six Strategies for War*.

Originally attributed to Jiang Shang, the brilliant strategist who helped establish the Western Zhou dynasty about 11th century BC, *Liu Tao* is now generally believed to have been written by an unknown recluse towards the end of the Warring States Era (475-221 BC).

There are more than 20 versions of *Liu Tao*. It is not uncommon for a major Chinese classic to have different versions, because through the ages, different copies have been passed down by different people. Some scholars, tempted to see their works being passed down, often adulterated famous classics with their own writings. In the present book, therefore, it is not surprising to find stories happening hundreds of years after the time the book was supposed to have been written.

The original text of *Liu Tao*, written in the form of conversations between Jiang Shang and King Wen and King Wu of Zhou, consists of 60 chapters in six articles totalling some 20,000 characters. The articles are named by different military strategies, and each deals with a principal subject.

The Civil Strategy discusses how, before a war, a state should build up its strength and make preparations. Among other things, it advocates meritocracy in official appointments and motivating the people by a system of generous reward and strict punishment.

The Military Strategy is about strategies to use against the enemy. For instance, before a war, one must make a comparative study of the strengths and weaknessses of both sides, so that the enemy may be defeated by attacking its most vulnerable point.

The Dragon Strategy is about military command and control. It stresses the importance of military command and strategic deployment on the battlefield. Apart from showing how orders can be issued and communicated, it also points out the importance of taking advantage of the natural elements.

The Tiger Strategy discusses the things to note when doing battle in open areas.

The Leopard Strategy, on the other hand, deals with the things to note when fighting in a narrow spot.

The last article, the Hound Strategy, discusses how foot soldiers, chariot troops, and cavalrymen can fight in coordination for maximum effectiveness.

In writing *Liu Tao*, the author drew on the experience and wisdom of Sun Zi, Confucius, Mencius, Han Fei Zi, Lao Zi, and Zhuang Zi. It was first translated into Japanese as early as the 16th century. Since then, the Japanese have widely translated, annotated, interpreted, commented on, and punctuated *Liu Tao* in more than 40 types of publication. The book has also been translated and published in Vietnam, North Korea, and other countries.

In many ways, the wisdom of ancient Chinese on the battlefield has applications in modern times. Indeed, Chinese classical military strategies are being widely reinterpreted and applied in the corporate world today, and a sound appreciation of these is *de rigueur* for many a sophisticated chief executive.

This cartoon interpretation of *Liu Tao* is by Wang Xuanming, a renowned cartoonist in the People's Republic of China.

Alan Chong

Contents

Introduction　總敍 1

The Civil Strategy　文韜 9
The art of recruiting talent and state management

The Military Strategy　武韜 60
The magic weapon for beating the enemy and building an empire

The Dragon Strategy　龍韜 85
The wisdom of military leadership

The Tiger Strategy　虎韜 137
The art of military manoeuvres

The Leopard Strategy　豹韜 175
The flexible strategy of striking the enemy at its weakest point

The Hound Strategy　犬韜 191
The secret of encircling and intercepting an enemy

Introduction

總敘

The last ruler of the Shang Dynasty (circa 16th - 11th century BC) was the despotic King Zhou.

1

Day and night, King Zhou would indulge in drinking and merrymaking with his favourite concubine, Da Ji, in his fabulous palaces and gardens.

Ha! Ha! Ha!

Hee! Hee! Hee!

Ho! Ho! Ho!

2

King Zhou also invented the *pao lao*, a cruel device on which his adversaries were seared to death.

What an ingenious gadget!

3

3

8

The Zhou clan, a tribe that lived in the northern reaches of the Wei River in present-day Shanxi province, was a vassal of the Shang state.

9

Yes, grandpa.

Remember, our state can become strong only if we get able people.

To prepare for the destruction of Shang, the Zhou tribe had been recruiting talent since the days of the grandfather of King Wen.

10

Jiang Shang, alias Jiang Ziya, was an able man living in the Zhou state.

My ancestors were high officials. But those were the days...

11

A child of a poor family, Jiang Shang worked as a butcher in Chaoge, the capital of the Shang Dynasty. Later, he opened a wineshop at Mengjin.

My talents have never been recognized in Shang.

12

I'm in my seventies now, but I still want a chance to prove my mettle.

13

News that King Wen was seeking able men prompted Jiang Shang to move to Mount Qi in Zhou.

14

We've been waiting for an able man like you for years!

King Wen was very happy when he found Jiang Shang.

15

Helped by Jiang Shang, a brilliant military strategist, King Wen first schemed to undermine the foundation of the Shang Dynasty. Then he destroyed the neighbouring states of Quanrong and Mixu.

16

The further states of Li, Yu, and Chong also fell in succession to the Zhou armies.

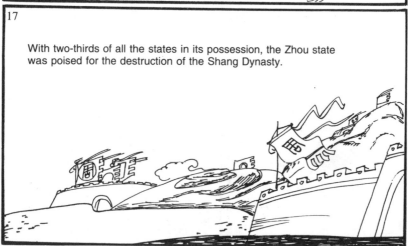

17

With two-thirds of all the states in its possession, the Zhou state was poised for the destruction of the Shang Dynasty.

20

At a decisive battle at Muye, the long-suffering slave soldiers of the Shang army revolted.

21

Faced with certain defeat, King Zhou fled back to the capital and burnt himself to death.

22

In helping King Wen and King Wu destroy the Shang Dynasty and establish the Zhou Dynasty, Jiang Shang proved himself a brilliant strategist. Using a format of conversations between the three men, *Liu Tao*, or *Six Strategies for War*, expounds the theories and principles of managing the state and the military, as well as methods of fighting a war. It has remained an inspiring work for centuries.

The
Civil
Strategy

文韜

The art of
recruiting
talent and state
management

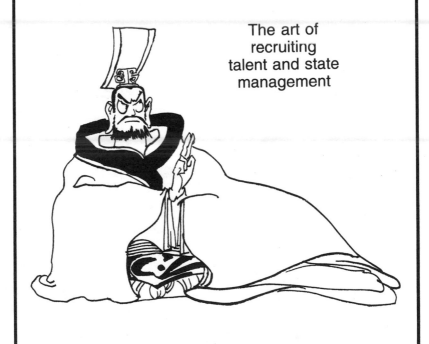

**A worthy man
fishes for
the world;
A mere mortal
fishes for fish
and prawns.**

To gain or to lose the world

16

**Control
personal desires,
respect others.**

4

Yao wore robes of rough materials even in winter...

5

... and ate only coarse rice and wild vegetables.

I'm happy just to have enough to eat every day.

6

To conform with nature's ways is to follow the workings of nature and uphold its laws.

Yao taught the people thus:

Sow in spring, work hard in summer, harvest in autumn, conserve and build up energy in winter.

During his 90-year rule, Yao controlled his personal desires, inspired his subjects by his virtues, and ruled in conformity with nature.

However, Yao's son Danzhu was undisciplined.

You've been on the throne long enough, Father. Move over and let me have a taste of being king.

Be strict with due reward and punishment irrespective of kinship.

1

I can't stand the arrogance and disrespect he shows his superiors.

2

But he's brave in battle and has scored many victories.

3

Even if it is someone you hate, you should reward him when reward is due.

This chest of gold is yours as a reward for your meritorious services.

12

Ma Su was sentenced to death.

I'm partly to blame for having picked you. But in the interest of Shu, I ought to punish you severely.

Please take care of my family, Prime Minister!

Give a lighter punishment when it is difficult to decide what punishment is due.

Scholars through the ages have placed much importance on the system of reward and punishment. Prominent scholar Su Dongpo said:

13

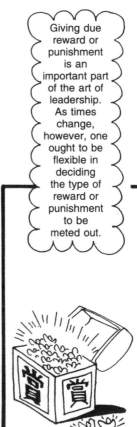

Giving due reward or punishment is an important part of the art of leadership. As times change, however, one ought to be flexible in deciding the type of reward or punishment to be meted out.

14

Give a greater reward when it is difficult to decide what reward is due.

The people desire that the state give more and take less.

Duke Jing of Qi asked Yan Zi after contemplating the scene from a high spot:

Who'll uphold the Qi state now that it has become so weak?

Yan Zi replied:

Tian Chengshi will.

Why?

He who gives generously to the people and wins their hearts gains the world. Tian Chengshi is doing just that.

5 Tian Chengshi used a big dipper for measuring grain he loaned out but used a small one for measuring grain in repayment.

Half will do!

Here's the five dippers of grain I borrowed last year.

6 Tian Chengshi took only a little meat after slaughtering an ox and distributed the rest to the people.

Let everyone have a taste of it.

7 He asked the ruler for higher pay for officials.

The duke's granted my request to triple your pay.

Thank you for your kindness.

27

12

There's hope yet, Your Majesty, if you change your policy.

13

Give generously to the people and win them over. How then can Tian Chengshi take away your state?

Benefits   Benefits

14

Asked about the way to rule a country, Jiang Shang said:

Give the people benefits and do not harm them; let them live in peace and do not kill indiscriminately. In short, take less from them and give them more.

Duke Jing did not heed the advice of Yan Zi and the Qi state eventually fell to Tian Chengshi. In present times, companies that provide excellent goods and services always do well. One of the reasons has to do with giving more to customers and taking less from them.

Dipper   Dipper

Foster good superior-subordinate relations.

1

A ruler should get close to his officials and speak humbly to prevent estrangement.

General, life will be tough on the way. Take care.

2

An official should be frank and sincere towards the ruler.

Fine. I appreciate your frankness and sincerity.

These are my views and proposals on Your Majesty's national policies. Please read them seriously.

3

Zhao Jianzi, the king of Jin who ruled during the Spring and Autumn Era, had two favourite white mules.

I'll never allow anyone to harm you!

30

It'd be uncaring of a ruler to sacrifice a general and let an animal live.

To do the opposite would be worthy of a benevolent ruler.

The king gave orders for one of his mules to be killed and its liver delivered to Xu Qu the same night.

Human life comes first!

That's no benevolence to me!

Soon after, in an attack on Zhai City led by the king, Xu Qu proved to be the bravest of the frontliners.

A superior treats his subordinates with kindheartedness and, in return, the subordinates submit sincerely to their superior. This traditional Chinese ethical value is still relevant today.

**Be humble
and fair
in dealing
with people.**

1

During the Spring and Autumn Era,
Zhao Jianzi, the king of Jin,
led an attack on the outer
city of the Wei state.

2

Zhao was
beating a
battle drum
behind a
big shield
far from
the
battlefront.

3

No matter how hard he beat the drum,
his soldiers just would not advance.

Dong
Dong
Dong

10 Under Duke Wen's leadership, the Jin army defeated the Chu army five times.

11 The Jin generals and soldiers who encircled the Wei state, conquered the Cao state, escorted Duke Xiang home, and triumphed at Dingba were the same troops that made up this army.

12 Aren't these facts enough proof that at times the fault lies not with the soldiers but with incompetent commanders?

13

Shocked into realization, Zhao Jianzi discarded the big shield and braved a hail of arrows and stones to take charge on the battlefront.

14

Inspired by the bravery of their commander, the Jin soldiers launched a bold assault and defeated the Wei defenders.

15

To hear a word from you is better than to gain a thousand chariots.

The basic reason for Zhao Jianzi's victory was his readiness to listen humbly to the criticisms of a subordinate and make timely corrections.

Nip trouble in the bud.

1

Tiny streams not stopped in time would converge into a torrential river.

2

A small flame not put out in time would grow into a ravaging fire.

A sapling not uprooted in time would grow into a mighty tree too hard to fell with an axe.

These phenomena show us that trouble can be easily nipped in the bud.

Towards the end of the Spring and Autumn Era, Zhi Bo of Jin gave fine horses and jade as gifts to the Wei state.

Nan Wenzi was very unhappy.

I'm really worried...

The king of Wei could not understand Nan Wenzi's reaction.

What's there to worry about when a large state like Jin takes the initiative to show its goodwill to me?

We ought to be on our guard when we receive a gift for no favour or service rendered.

Fine horses and jade are usually given by a small state to a big state as a tribute. But now Jin is doing the opposite...

Just a small gift, don't mention it.

10

Isn't Zhi Bo's gesture suspicious and worrying?

You're right. Beef up the border defences at once.

11

True enough, Zhi Bo launched a sneak attack, thinking that Wei would be caught off guard after receiving the gifts.

12

But finding Wei well guarded, Zhi Bo retreated in failure.

A wise man in Wei has seen through my ploy. Let's go home!

Keen observation and accurate judgement are vital to averting calamities.

A happy people is a requisite for national prosperity.

1

A ruler's duty is to make the country and its people prosperous as quickly as possible.

I shall strive to raise wages and lower prices...

2

A secure and contented people is receptive to the teachings of ethics and would not think of rebelling.

3

During the Spring and Autumn Era, King Zhuang of Chu thought of conquering the Chen state.

Go to the Chen state and assess their defence.

Yes.

42

The Chen state is far from impregnable.

Ha! Ha! Ha!...

The huge revenue collected by such a small state must have been extorted from its people. They must surely hate their king.

The high city walls and deep moat must have cost a huge sum and placed a great burden on the people.

The citizens are overworked and heavily taxed...

Wall building!

Moat dredging!

Conscription!

12

The suffering people of Chen are definitely unwilling to die for their despotic king.

13

With this understanding, the Chu army launched an attack on the city. The Chen state fell with little resistance.

14

Jiang Shang said:

When the people are poor, they are unamenable to the precepts of ethics. Without moral values, social cohesion is impossible, and the loss of the people's support will spell downfall for the state.

History has shown that dynasties whose people were allowed to live and work in peace and contentment enjoyed prolonged peace. The Qin and Sui dynasties, which taxed the people harshly to finance their lavish building projects, fell quickly.

**Show true grit
in calamity.**

Fan Sui was originally an official of Wei during the Warring States Era. Persecuted by the Wei premier, he fled to Qin.

The constant state of war during the time gave Fan Sui an opportunity to show his talents, which soon caught the eye of King Zhao of Qin.

Wonderful! I'll make you a high official.

Adopt this policy and you will achieve hegemony.

Befriend distant states and attack those nearby.

45

3

Marquis Rang of Qin attacked the Han state ten times but failed to capture it.

4

Fan Sui said to King Zhao:

Did Marquis Rang fail because Qin is weak and Han is strong?

5

In a war, some people advocate killing enemy generals and soldiers as the main aim.

AAAh!

6

Some people advocate seizing enemy territories as the main aim.

All these lands are ours now!

Since rulers are fond of territorial expansion, generals are happy seizing land for them.

We've secured another 500 square miles of land in this campaign.

Well done! A double payrise for you.

Fan Sui added:

Seizing land without destroying enemy troops is the reason why we couldn't win.

If we concentrated on eliminating enemy troops instead of seizing their land, we'd be able to destroy Han in a few years.

10

Kill!
Kill!
Kill!

King Zhao accepted Fan Sui's proposal and inflicted heavy casualties on the Han army. The Han state fell quickly.

11

In adversity, the survival of the weak is constantly being threatened. Those who have the courage to accept challenges and give full play to their potential may turn out to be heroes, as many the likes of Fan Sui have done in their time.

12

Many youths of our time are used to a life of plenty and enjoyment from an early age. In such an environment, it is difficult to nurture outstanding talent.

Endless wars and harsh living conditions during the Spring and Autumn Era and the Warring States Era have produced numerous heroes. The reasons for their emergence should give food for thought to people with high aspirations.

48

**Meritocracy
is the way to
prolonged prosperity.**

1

A wise ruler would employ people judiciously and give key positions to worthy and honest gentlemen, thus making the nation strong.

2

Sweetie, I'll make your dad the prime minister, your brother the commander...

Hee! Hee!

But a fatuous ruler would let ill-behaved, dishonest, and hypocritical villains occupy key positions and cause the nation to decline.

3

During the Spring and Autumn Era, the Chu army suffered a series of defeats at the hands of the Wu army, which pursued them right to the suburbs of the Chu capital.

4

Five officials remonstrated with He Lu, the king of Wu:

It's unwise to fight the Chu army deep inside their territory. We recommend retreating at once.

?!

5

He Lu summoned his trusted official Wu Zixu for advice.

Advance or retreat?

6

Wu Zixu said:

Those officials are cowards. Retreat would mean losing a golden opportunity.

51

A unified command and unified action are prerequisites for military success.

1

King Huang said:

An army acting in unison under a unified command is an effective elite force.

2

A coalition army was attacking the Zheng state.

There're soldiers all over! We're doomed!

3

The coalition army had an obvious military advantage.

The Zheng state is doomed!

**A person is bound
to have one form
of worry or another.**

1

The despotic King Zhou was not a fool. He was in fact intelligent and sharp.

2

Many who remonstrated with him were rendered speechless by his dialectical prowess.

You've any more to say?

3

A man of extraordinary strength, he could subdue fierce animals with his bare hands.

Surrender?

4

The Shang Dynasty had been in existence for 600 years and King Zhou had able men like Ji Zi, Wei Zi, and Bi Gan.

5

But King Zhou's 700,000-strong army was no match for King Wu's army of 50,000 men at the decisive battle at Muye.

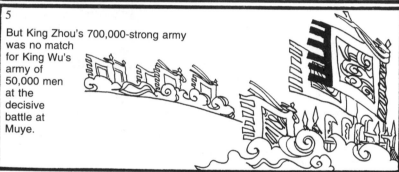

6

King Zhou failed because he didn't realize his once-strong country was on the brink of collapse.

Jiang Shang said:

7

He only cared about enjoyment and failed to see the imminent disaster.

Arrogant and short-sighted, he did not care about military training.

Hee! Hee! Ha! Ha!

His Majesty's busy!

Military Training Plan

8

9

He treated his loyal officials cruelly.

10

Most of his soldiers were untrained slaves who could not withstand an attack.

I never thought I'd be left alone so soon!

Nothing in the world remains unchanged. Survival and death, good times and bad alternate. Without anticipating disasters and preparing for them, a good time will soon be gone.

The Military Strategy

武韜

The magic weapon
for beating
the enemy and
building an empire

The superior strategy is to win with wit.

1

Jiang Shang said:

A victory secured by force isn't a perfect victory.

2

Could there be such a wonderful thing, or are you dreaming?

A powerful army is one that suffers no casualties; a perfect victory is one secured without fierce battles.

3 During the Warring States Era, General Zhao Yang of Chu won a war against Wei.

Qi will be my next target!

4 High official Chen Zhen said to a fearful king of Qi:

I can persuade the Chu state to withdraw their forces without using a single soldier.

A pay rise for you if you succeed.

5. Hee! Hee!

General, congratulations on your splendid victory over the Wei state. You're indeed a military genius!

Chen Zhen saw Zhao Yang in Chu.

6 What official rank will you be given under Chu laws for such a huge victory?

7 *Shang zhuguo*.*

* The second highest military post in the Chu state.

He who wins over the people gains the world.

Jiang Shang said:

The world doesn't belong to one man but to all.

The quest for the world is like the hunt for an animal in that everyone covets a share of the quarry.

Tiger Bone Wine

3 The quest for the world is also like crossing a river in the same boat in that everyone gets a share of the benefits if the crossing is successful.

4 If the crossing fails, everyone suffers.

5 King Zhuang of Chu led an attack on Song.

6 But the Chu forces failed to capture Song after several assaults.

Set up camps and encircle the city.

Yes!

Winning by surprise and secrecy of action plans

72

**The will of
the people is
like water.**

4

The last ruler of the Xia Dynasty was Jie, the decadent despot much hated by his people.

5

Shang, an eastern vassal state, was growing in strength. King Tang of Shang was waiting for a chance to destroy Xia.

I need to join forces with other vassals. But how can I gain their trust and support?

6

On an outing, King Tang saw a farmer catching birds with nets in the forest.

After spreading his nets in all four directions, the farmer knelt and prayed:

May all the flying birds above and walking animals below fall into my nets.

The encounter gave King Tang an inspiration.

!

He broke into tears and said:

Only King Jie can be so cruel as to try to catch everything in his nets.

Remove the nets in three directions, leaving only one.

11

King Tang also knelt and prayed:

All birds and animals wishing to go east, go east; wishing to go west, go west; wishing to fly up, fly up. Let only those that do not want to obey heaven's wishes come into my net.

12

You must be kind even to animals; don't kill them all.

After praying, King Tang told the farmer and his officials:

13

Only a few do not obey heaven's wishes and it's our duty to catch them.

**Defeat a
powerful opponent
by praising him.**

1

Qi attacked Song. King Zhao of Yan told General Zhang Kui:

A flatterer.

Qi is a strong state. The King of Qi will be happy if you reinforce him with our troops.

2

But the king of Qi killed General Zhang with an excuse.

The chap looks like a spy in every way.

What a worthless death for me!

3

King Zhao sobbed bitterly upon getting the news.

I sincerely sent our troops to help Qi but its king has killed our general instead. Attack Qi at once!

I shall not fail you, Your Majesty!

8

But in what way do I not seem wise?

Your Majesty should give up attacking Qi.

Then send an envoy to Qi...

Fine, fine!

10

The king of Qi was drinking with his officials when the Yan envoy arrived.

Hng!

The king of Yan has sent me here to ask Your Majesty's forgiveness!

11

Zhang Kui deserved death for insubordination and our king said he was partly to blame for this.

12

His Majesty is a worthy king. Why else didn't he kill envoys of other states but ours?

Our king said:

13

It was all my fault for not choosing the right person. Now I'm sending an envoy who knows protocol well to ask His Majesty's forgiveness.

Our king also said:

17

From then on, Qi relaxed its vigilance against Yan. When Yan grew stronger, it attacked Qi, captured more than 70 cities, and pushed it to the brink of total collapse.

18

The way to undermine a powerful opponent is to inflate his ego and make him more arrogant and complacent.

Keep your opponent's weak points concealed and praise his strong points to blunt his sense of self-judgement. Let him go to battle blindly with his weaknesses and you will defeat him easily.

The Dragon Strategy

龍韜

The wisdom of
military leadership

Arrogate all authority to oneself but pool the wisdom of the masses.

1

A general needs the support of many aides to have full control of his troops.

He needs five advisers, three astronomers, three geographers, nine military strategists, and personnel in logistics, intelligence, etc – a total of more than 70 people.

2

However, he can have only one trusted aide for the military master plan that decides his fate.

General

3

Not only must I have full control of the situation, but I must also keep cool in an emergency.

Trusted Aide

During the struggle for supremacy between Chu and Han in the final years of the Qin Dynasty, Liu Bang, the king of Han, was plagued by a serious shortage of food for his troops.

Your Majesty, we're running out of rice again.

Adviser Li Sheng offered an idea:

In the past, King Tang of Shang gave land to descendants of King Jie, whom he vanquished; King Wu did likewise after defeating King Zhou of Shang.

But descendants of the six states conquered by Qin were left without an inch of land.

If Your Majesty could give official ranks to descendants of the six states, the people would certainly be grateful for Your Majesty's kindness.

12

King Tang and King Wu could afford to be generous because they were sure of defeating their opponents.
But are you sure you are able to defeat Xiang Yu of Chu now?

Zhang Liang explained:

13

Your followers are motivated by prospects of officialship when you succeed in establishing your dynasty.

OFFICIAL SEAL

14

If the six states were revived and their descendants made kings, your followers would leave.

I've been offered the premiership of Qi. Goodbye!

I'll be the chief general of Zhao. Bye bye!

15

Who then would Your Majesty depend on to help you gain the world?

90

Victory or defeat depends on the judicious employment of people.

1

A shrewd general must be able to employ people judiciously, and take full advantage of their talents.

2

In the power struggle between Chu and Han, Liu Bang prevailed because he allowed his followers to give their talents full play.

Han Dynasty scholar Yang Xiong said:

3

His archrival, Xiang Yu, was a formidable but foolhardy fighter who could not make full use of his followers.

I'm the world's No.1; others are useless!

91

As a military strategist, Liu Bang was no match for Zhang Liang.

As a military commander, he paled in comparison with Han Xin.

As a state administrator, he was not as effective as Xiao He.

But Liu Bang was able to use these people judiciously by giving them suitable positions.

I hope all of you will do your best in your jobs!

7

Appointment

In the power struggle at the end of the Han Dynasty, Yuan Shao was a strong contender with many able strategists and generals.

8

9

But he lacked the capability to make use of talent.

Shall I send Zhang San or Li Si?

10

Strategists Tian Feng and Ju Shou offered him ideas.

93

But they ended up in jail.

Put these two guys in jail to sober up. That's the best position for them.

Yes!

11

Xu You, Zhang He, and Gao Lan were forced to join the camp of Cao Cao when they were suspected of being spies.

Welcome, gentlemen!

12

Despite his superior military strength, Yuan Shao was defeated by Cao Cao. Ashamed, he finally died of an illness.

13

Picking and using talent judiciously are important not only in warfare but also in any undertaking.

Scrutinize a person carefully before appointing him to an important position.

A commanding general is vital to the survival of a country in any war.

The choice of a commanding general should therefore be made only after very careful screening.

3

During the Warring States Era, Su Dai went to Qi as a spy for Yan and won the trust of the Qi ruler.

I like you. You've given me a lot of good ideas.

Hee! Hee!

4

I've managed to drive a wedge between Qi and Zhao. It's time to invade Qi.

Su Dai sent someone to report back to the king of Yan.

Su Dai said:

5

The king of Yan immediately ordered an attack on Qi.

Kill!

Kill!

6

The Yan troops wanted to attack Qi but got bogged down in Jin territory. This shows they're weak and indecisive.

Meanwhile, Su Dai got a canvasser to talk to the king of Qi.

7

The canvasser went on to tout for Su Dai.

With his talents, Su Dai should be able to lead the Qi army to a resounding victory against the Yan invaders. When Qi triumphs over Yan, Zhao will also submit to Your Majesty...

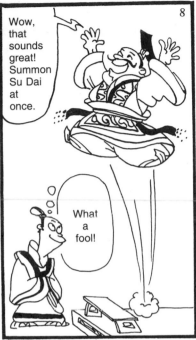

8

Wow, that sounds great! Summon Su Dai at once.

What a fool!

9

Su Dai pretended to refuse modestly.

I think Your Majesty should appoint another person!

I want you to be the army commander in the war against Yan!

APPOINT- MENT

10

But the king insisted.

You just go ahead. I'll understand.

11

The Qi army, of course, was soundly beaten and suffered more than 20,000 casualties.

The king of Qi 12 was unperturbed.

Su Dai said he's let Your Majesty down and asked to be punished.

This is my fault. I still think Su Dai is a rare talent.

13

Once again, Su Dai sent a canvasser to the king of Qi.

Go tell the king; he's bound to believe you.

Do not judge a person by his appearance.

102

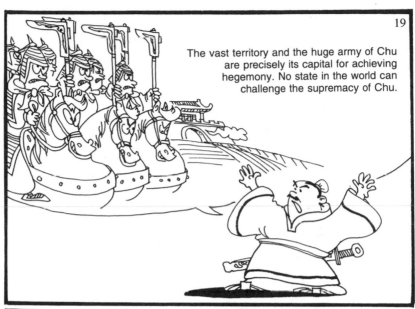

19

The vast territory and the huge army of Chu are precisely its capital for achieving hegemony. No state in the world can challenge the supremacy of Chu.

20

Qin is just an infantile state. But its army has humiliated Chu on three occasions.

21

This is indeed a great insult to the people of Chu. Even we, the people of Zhao, feel humiliated. But Your Majesty doesn't seem to take it to heart.

22

An alliance of Zhao and Chu will benefit both states.

I think you're right. I agree to a common front against Qin.

23

An oath of alliance was taken immediately.

24

Upon returning to Zhao, Ping Yuanjun immediately made Mao Sui an esteemed hanger-on.

Never again will I judge a person by his appearance.

Did I look like an awl this time, master?

Do not judge a book by its cover. This is especially true when picking an able man whose looks often belie his true talents. That's why it takes someone with an extraordinary acumen to identify talents.

Do not doubt subordinates entrusted with important positions.

4 When Qin attacked Qi during the Warring States Era, the king of Qi appointed Zhang Zi as commander in chief of the army.

The survival of Qi is now in your hands!

Zhang Zi acted suspiciously; he secretly changed our army banners to those of Qin.

5 Scouts kept the king informed about frontline happenings.

6 The king did not show any reaction.

7 After a while, the same scout came and reported:

Zhang Zi might have surrendered.

108

110

The key to establishing authority

1

A commanding general establishes his authority by executing offenders even though they may be of high positions, and shows his virtue by rewarding meritorious achievers even though they may be of low positions.

2

Execution and reward are two key aspects of commandership.

REWARD

EXECUTION

3

Feng Changqing was a strict military disciplinary officer under General Gao Xianzhi of the Tang Dynasty.

Zheng Dequan, you're setting a bad example by blatantly flouting the rules.

Hng!

112

113

115

116

**Fight ahead of
your soldiers and
you will lead an
all-conquering army.**

1

A brilliant commander can inspire his soldiers to fight selflessly in battle.

2

What made you so game?

Our commander went through thick and thin with us.

Before General Tian Dan of Qi left for an attack on Di City, Lu Zhonglian told him:

You won't succeed; you might as well stay put.

3

118

8

Lu Zhonglian said:

You were humble and fearless when you fought against the Yan army.

9

You were ready to die for the state.

Fight for our survival! If we lose, we'll die! There's no other way out!

10

Inspired by your selflessness, the soldiers fought resolutely.

Charge!

11

That was why Qi could defeat Yan. But now, you're different.

12

You have cities to enjoy and land taxes to collect.

Secrecy is of paramount importance.

1. A ruler and his commander use eight different types of tally to ensure secrecy in their communications.

2. To the enemy, the tallies mean nothing.

I don't know. My job is just to deliver it.

What the heck is this?

3. But to the communicating parties...

Ha! Ha! General Zhang's captured another two enemy generals!

4.

The king's ordering us to seize the enemy city!

123

15

Hou Sheng also recommended a strong man, Zhu Hai, to the prince.

If General Jin refuses to hand over military power after seeing the tally, he can kill him for you.

That's great!

16 The prince met General Jin.

The king asks you to hand over the commandership of your troops.

That's the king's order all right, but...

17

Zhu Hai killed the hesitant general.

General Jin has been executed for defying the king's order. I now order you to attack the Qin army!

Secrecy is a double-edged sword that cuts both ways. Leaked to and exploited by an opponent, it can also do great damage to oneself. Prince Xin Ling cleverly exploited this fact.

Seize the opportunity and act decisively.

King Zhou, the last ruler of the Shang Dynasty, alienated his officials and subjects by his despotism.

Waa!

I've the patent for this *pao lao* device.

The time was ripe for the Zhou clan on the west to destroy the Shang Dynasty.

What's the situation in Shang?

King Wu asked his spy:

The good people have left and the masses dare not speak up.

5

Jiang Shang said:

The Shang state's on the brink of total collapse. It's time to attack it.

6

King Wu set off with a powerful army.

7

After passing through a tunnel, King Wu would order it sealed.

8

After crossing a river, the king would order the ships destroyed.

9

After crossing a bridge, the king would order it demolished.

The winner is endowed with a keen sense of judgement.

During the Spring and Autumn Era, a coalition army of Jin, Lu, and other states attacked Qi.

The Qi army set up a defence line at Pingyang. Duke Ling went on a hill to watch the movements of the Jin army in the distance.

What an impressive army with rows of chariots and numerous soldiers and generals!

Frightened by the battle array of the Jin army, Duke Ling fled home, leaving his army behind.

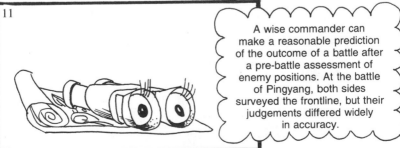

4
The palace was completed according to Dong's specifications despite objections from other officials.
5
Zhao Xiangzi succeeded Zhao Jianzi upon his death. Zhi Bo, the most powerful of the ministers, tried to gain sole control of Jin.
Tell the families of Han, Wei, and Zhao to give me a piece of their land each or I'll get tough with them.
6
Several days later...
The Hans and Weis have agreed to give these lands to you, sir.
7
Zhao Xiangzi says his land isn't fertile enough and he'd like to get some from you.
Audacious fool!

135

The
Tiger
Strategy

虎韜

The art
of military
manoeuvres

Favourable weather conditions, topographic advantages, and the people's support are the magic weapons in warfare.

139

140

10

The Lu soldiers were surprised by the armed intruders, who proceeded to take the city.

11

During the Spring and Autumn Era, Zhi Bo of Jin wanted to attack Yao, a small state nestling on steep mountains. But there was no access road.

12

An idea flashed through his mind and he summoned his blacksmith.

Make a huge bell like this at once!

18
Would the greedy, untrustworthy Zhi Bo leave a bell here for nothing?
19
He must be thinking of attacking us and using this bell as a bait.
20
When we get the road ready and bring the bell home, the Jin army will follow right behind!
21
But the king insisted on having the bell. Nine days after the bell was brought to Yao, Zhi Bo's army came through the new road and destroyed Yao.
In warfare, it is vital to consider all human and environmental factors and use all available advantages against the enemy.

Bravery is the prerequisite for getting out of a tight spot.

To break through an enemy encirclement, you need good weapons; but above all, you need bravery.

A fearless army is all-conquering.

Towards the end of the Qin Dynasty, Xiang Yu of Chu rebelled against Qin but was heavily defeated by the Qin army at the battle of Dingtao.

145

Realizing it was a matter of life and death, the Chu generals and soldiers fought resolutely and finally defeated the Qin army after nine fierce battles.

With the surrender of the Qin commander, the main force of the Qin army was destroyed.

Soldiers fighting regardless of their lives to break out of a desperate situation can take on ten times their number of enemies. In such circumstances, bravery is a decisive factor.

Material preparation is vital for success.

1

Soldiers must be well-trained in the use of weapons.

1, 2, 3; left, right, left.

2 With a complete stockpile of war materials, the commander has little to worry about.

Now, I can relax.

3 Towards the end of the Warring States Era, chariot-based combat tactics could no longer meet the demands of expanded warfare involving large numbers of troops and vast territories.

Oh no, not again!

8 Many conservative officials objected to the king's ideas.

9 Ignoring objections from various quarters, the king led his soldiers in cavalry warfare training.

10 Finally, with an elite cavalry force, Zhao was able to beat off the Xiongnu invaders from the north, capture Yan and Qi in the east, and challenge the supremacy of Qin in the west.

Surprise the enemy and go for the jugular.

152

153

**Laxity
will result
in failure.**

1

Soldiers must be constantly on guard to defend a city.

Commander, the enemy has stormed into the city!

2

Laxity is the root cause of failure.

They've gone to play *mahjong*!

Where are the sentries?

3

I want to attack Zhongshan. Go there, survey the situation and report to me.

During the Warring States Era, King Wuling of Zhao said to official Li Ci:

155

4

On his return, Li Ci said:

Your Majesty can attack Zhongshan right away. If Zhao doesn't, Qi or Yan will be the first bird to catch the worm.

5

Why?

6

The king of Zhongshan likes recluses and gives them lots of concessions. He often visits them in remote areas with officials.

7

Doesn't that make him a worthy king who respects the learned? How does that make Zhongshan vulnerable?

158

Maintain friendly ties and strive to win sincere support.

When Qin grew in strength towards the end of the Warring States Era, the other six states, Qi, Yan, Han, Chu, Zhao, and Wei, were afraid of Qin's aggression.

12 I've calculated that, together, the six states in Shandong have five times the area of Qin and 10 times its military strength. If the six states join forces, they'll be more than a match for Qin.

13 Some people advocate suing for peace by ceding territories to Qin. This will only make it stronger and eventually all six states will become easy game for it.

14 Therefore, I strongly urge Your Majesty to form an alliance with the other five states against Qin.

15 The king of Zhao accepted the proposal and gave Su Qin a large sum of money for his mission.

Please sell your idea to the other states.

Winning by benevolence

In the final year of the Qin Dynasty, Liu Bang, leader of one of the rebel factions, was pressing towards the Qin capital of Xianyang while Xiang Yu, another faction leader, fought a decisive battle with the main forces of Qin elsewhere.

4

5

The king of Qin, Ziying, made Yao Pass the last ditch.

6

7

Yes, yes, of course!

Surrender to our forces tomorrow at the bank of the Ba River. Don't forget to bring along your royal seal.

Liu Bang sent an official to tell Ziying to surrender.

8

Seeing no hope of saving the situation, Ziying surrendered as he was told.

9

When Liu Bang entered Xianyang with his troops, he was fascinated by the fabulous Qin palace.

Wonderful! I must move in and enjoy myself.

10

You mustn't move in or touch the treasures here if you want to win the people's hearts.

Fan Kuai and Zhang Liang said:

15 Liu Bang's actions won the support of the people of the territories he took over.

16 Shortly thereafter, Xiang Yu marched into Xianyang with his troops after defeating the main forces of Qin.

17 First, he put Ziying to death.

It's my turn to be king!

Sorry! It's my boss' order!

Spare me, please! I'm just an ordinary man now.

Xiang Yu allowed his generals and soldiers to plunder the city and kill wantonly.

18

19

He also set fire to the Xianyang Palace, which burned for three months.

20

If you don't listen, Xiang Yu will come. He's worse than a demon!

His actions cost him the support of the people.

Despite being a mighty warrior, Xiang Yu ended up committing suicide after failing in the struggle for power. It was the loss of the people's support that caused his downfall.

Know your enemy's plans before you devise countermeasures.

171

The Leopard Strategy

豹韜

The flexible strategy
of striking the enemy
at its weakest point

Attack is active defence.

1

In the final year of the Western Jin Dynasty, warlord Shi Le was encircled in Xiang Guo by Western Jin troops.

2

Outnumbered, Shi Le was in a desperate situation.

We can't fight them. We can only concentrate on defence.

3

General Zhang Bin and General Kong Chang said:

Passive defence will only lead to defeat.

4

"Charging doors" are tunnels dug through the city wall but concealed from the enemy's view. During an attack, soldiers would quickly puncture the wall and charge out.

The weakest part of the encirclement is in the northern city gate. If we prepare dozens of "charging doors" in the city wall and let our troops charge out in a surprise attack...

5

Shi Le adopted the proposal. First he ordered his men to make a lot of noises on the city wall.

Waa!
Waa!
Ho!
Ho!
Charge!
Charge!
Kill!
Kill!

!

6

Kill!

Charge!

Waa!

The noises attracted the attention of the Western Jin soldiers.

What's that nonsense?

7

Charge!
Charge!

Soldiers hidden in the tunnels broke out suddenly and took the enemy troops by surprise. Shi Le led his troops in hot pursuit and scored a major victory.

8

When one is attacked by a strong opponent, passive defence only brings disaster on oneself. Only a defence stratagem that includes a swift counterattack plan is an effective one.

When facing a strong opponent, a rapid counterattack often gives surprisingly good results.

**Variability
is the essence of
military strategy.**

1

Birds gather and
disperse in infinite
variations.

2

Clouds, too, gather and
disperse in infinite variations.

3

Likewise,
military
stratagems
have to vary
according to
battleground
conditions.

Yu Wentai's subordinates were against his proposal to attack Dou Tai.

We're facing the enemy's main force. It'd be dangerous to attack Dou Tai at the expense of our defence here.

8

With his troops poised for an attack, Gao Huan must be thinking we'd concentrate on our defence here and Dou Tai would never expect an attack from us.

9

Yu Wentai stood his ground.

10

It'll take me only five days to defeat Dou Tai. I don't think Gao Huan would have even finished his floating bridges by then.

11

Yu Wentai sneaked off
with 6,000 light cavalry troops
and took only two days and nights
to arrive at Tong Pass.

12

Dou Tai never thought much
of the attackers.

Cross the
river and
teach these
Western Wei
soldiers a
good lesson!

13

Before Dou Tai's troops could organize
themselves, they came under
fierce attack from the
well-prepared Western
Wei soldiers.

183

**Having more
men is not always
an advantage.**

Having more
men is usually
an advantage in
a battle but not
in a narrow place.

A small army is no
match for a large
army in a direct clash.
But it still could win by
taking advantage of its
agility in an ambush.

First, find out the
enemy's weak point
and exploit it. Then
create a battle
environment
advantageous
to our side.

Yu Wentai ordered most of his men to hide
themselves in the thick reeds,
allowing only a small number to be seen.

18

Seeing only
a few men,
Gao Huan's troops
scrambled for what
they thought was easy prey.
This put their battle array
in chaos.

19 Just then, Yu Wentai's hidden troops sprang out in an ambush.

20 Troops led by Li Bi charged in and split the Eastern Wei soldiers into two isolated groups.

Come and help us quickly!

I'm sorry! We're in trouble too!

21 Defeated again, Gao Huan rode off sadly.

To win as an underdog, one must identify the enemy's weak point and exploit it.

The Hound Strategy

犬韜

The secret
of encircling
and intercepting
an enemy

Choosing an opportune moment for an attack

1

Be careful in choosing the right moment for an attack.

Don't attack now. The time isn't ripe yet.

2

According to my study, there are 14 circumstances under which an attack can be launched:

3

When the enemy forces have just gathered; when the enemy soldiers and horses are hungry; when the weather is foul...

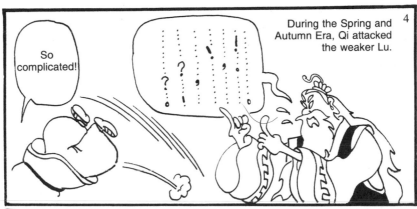

So complicated!

During the Spring and Autumn Era, Qi attacked the weaker Lu.

Battle lines were drawn at Changshao. The Qi forces sounded battle drums for advance.

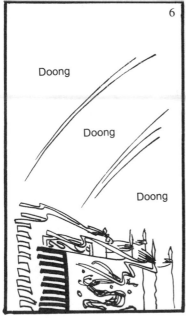

Doong

Doong

Doong

Hold it!

Duke Zhuang of Lu was stopped by strategist Cao Gui when he wanted to beat the drum too.

194

12 The Lu ruler was again stopped by Cao Gui when he wanted to order a pursuit of the Qi army.

Hold it!

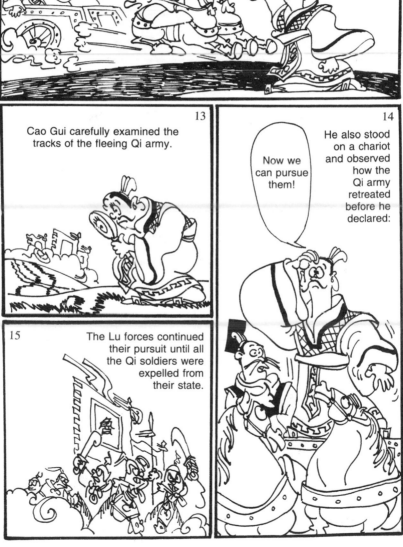

13 Cao Gui carefully examined the tracks of the fleeing Qi army.

14 He also stood on a chariot and observed how the Qi army retreated before he declared:

Now we can pursue them!

15 The Lu forces continued their pursuit until all the Qi soldiers were expelled from their state.

**Strength
comes from
rigorous training.**

7 Shoot!

The people immediately took up archery and practised hard.

8 In time, everyone became a crack shot.

I've already shot through the bull's-eye!

I never miss in 1,000 shots!

I never miss in 100 shots!

9 When the Qin army attacked again, the people of Shangdi easily beat them off with their deadly shots.

A wise commander would train his soldiers rigorously in combat skills. This is the best way to raise the battle power of the army.

An army should use its resources judiciously.

1

The chariot is useful in charging, intercepting, and encircling enemy troops.

2

The cavalry is useful in tracking and pursuing enemy troops.

3

The type of military equipment and soldiers to use should be suited to the battleground conditions.

For about 1,600 years from the Xia Dynasty to the Spring and Autumn Era, soldiers fought only on chariots.

This is a long-established military machine!

4

The chariot was clumsy, heavy, and difficult to drive. Moreover, its use was severely restricted by the battleground terrain.

Hey, let's level the battleground so that our chariots can run.

That's a huge job, buddy!

5

By the Warring States Era, the advent of iron weapons and improvements in archery equipment made foot soldiers and the cavalry effective weapons against chariot attacks.

Chariots are nothing to fear!

6

7

With several choices available, the commander had to consider carefully which type of soldiers to use in a battle.

Which type of soldiers shall I send?

8

General Wei Shu of Jin of the Spring and Autumn Era was the first Han general to break away from conventional chariot warfare tactics in the battle against the Wuzhong state.

The Wuzhong army consists of foot soldiers and we're using chariots.

9

The rugged battleground terrain is unsuitable for chariot warfare.

In such terrain, ten foot soldiers can defeat a chariot.

10

If we turn our troops into foot soldiers, we'll be able to trap the enemy in the difficult terrain.

11

12

Good idea!

So I suggest giving up the chariots from now on.

13

A stubborn general who refused to join the foot-soldier army unit was executed to serve as a deterrent to others.

I'll rather die than be a foot soldier!

14

The Jin army organized itself into five regiments.

15

The Wuzhong soldiers had never seen the new battle formation of the Jin army.

16

While they were wondering what tactic to adopt, the Jin soldiers charged and defeated them.

A commander should be familiar with the nature of military resources available to him and pick the right ones to use to his advantage in a battle.

A Brief Chronology of Chinese History

夏 Xia Dynasty			About 2100 – 1600 BC
商 Shang Dynasty			About 1600 – 1100 BC
周 Zhou Dynasty	西周 Western Zhou Dynasty		About 1100 – 771 BC
	東周 Eastern Zhou Dynasty		770 – 256 BC
	春秋 Spring and Autumn Period		770 – 476 BC
	戰國 Warring States		475 – 221 BC
秦 Qin Dynasty			221 – 207 BC
漢 Han Dynasty	西漢 Western Han		206 BC – AD 24
	東漢 Eastern Han		25 – 220
三國 Three Kingdoms	魏 Wei		220 – 265
	蜀漢 Shu Han		221 – 263
	吳 Wu		222 – 280
西晉 Western Jin Dynasty			265 – 316
東晋 Eastern Jin Dynasty			317 – 420
南北朝 Northern and Southern Dynasties	南朝 Southern Dynasties	宋 Song	420 – 479
		齊 Qi	479 – 502
		梁 Liang	502 – 557
		陳 Chen	557 – 589
	北朝 Northern Dynasties	北魏 Northern Wei	386 – 534
		東魏 Eastern Wei	534 – 550
		北齊 Northern Qi	550 – 577
		西魏 Western Wei	535 – 556
		北周 Northern Zhou	557 – 581
隋 Sui Dynasty			581 – 618
唐 Tang Dynasty			618 – 907
五代 Five Dynasties	後梁 Later Liang		907 – 923
	後唐 Later Tang		923 – 936
	後晋 Later Jin		936 – 946
	後漢 Later Han		947 – 950
	後周 Later Zhou		951 – 960
宋 Song Dynasty	北宋 Northern Song Dynasty		960 – 1127
	南宋 Southern Song Dynasty		1127 – 1279
遼 Liao Dynasty			916 – 1125
金 Jin Dynasty			1115 – 1234
元 Yuan Dynasty			1271 – 1368
明 Ming Dynasty			1368 – 1644
清 Qing Dynasty			1644 – 1911
中華民國 Republic of China			1912 – 1949
中華人民共和國 People's Republic of China			1949 –

Strategy & Leadership Series by Wang Xuanming

Thirty-six Stratagems: Secret Art of War
Translated by Koh Kok Kiang (cartoons) &
Liu Yi (text of the stratagems)
A Chinese military classic which emphasizes deceptive schemes to achieve military objectives. It has attracted the attention of military authorities and general readers alike.

Six Strategies for War: The Practice of Effective Leadership
Translated by Alan Chong
A powerful book for rulers, administrators and leaders, it covers critical areas in management and warfare including: how to recruit talents and manage the state; how to beat the enemy and build an empire; how to lead wisely; and how to manoeuvre brilliantly.

Gems of Chinese Wisdom: Mastering the Art of Leadership
Translated by Leong Weng Kam
Wise up with this delightful collection of tales and anecdotes on the wisdom of great men and women in Chinese history, including Confucius, Meng Changjun and Gou Jian.

Three Strategies of Huang Shi Gong: The Art of Government
Translated by Alan Chong
Reputedly one of man's oldest monograph on military strategy, it unmasks the secrets behind brilliant military manoeuvres, clever deployment and control of subordinates, and effective government.

100 Strategies of War: Brilliant Tactics in Action
Translated by Yeo Ai Hoon
The book captures the essence of extensive military knowledge and practice, and explores the use of psychology in warfare, the importance of building diplomatic relations with the enemy's neighbours, the use of espionage and reconnaissance, etc.

Asiapac Comic Series (by Tsai Chih Chung)

Art of War
Translated by Leong Weng Kam

The Art of War provides a compact set of principles essential for victory in battles; applicable to military strategists, in business and human relationships.

Book of Zen
Translated by Koh Kok Kiang

Zen makes the art of spontaneous living the prime concern of the human being. Tsai depicts Zen with unfettered versatility; his illustrations spans a period of more than 2,000 years.

Da Xue
Translated by Mary Ng En Tzu

The second book in the Four Books of the Confucian Classics. It sets forth the higher principles of moral science and advocates that the cultivation of the person be the first thing attended to in the process of the pacification of kingdoms.

Fantasies of the Six Dynasties
Translated by Jenny Lim

Tsai Chih Chung has creatively illustrated and annotated 19 bizarre tales of human encounters with supernatural beings which were compiled during the Six Dyansties (AD 220-589).

Lun Yu
Translated by Mary Ng En Tzu

A collection of the discourses of Confucius, his disciples and others on various topics. Several bits of choice sayings have been illustrated for readers in this book.

New Account of World Tales
Translated by Alan Chong

These 120 selected anecdotes tell the stories of emperors, princes, high officials, generals, courtiers, urbane monks and lettered gentry of a turbulent time. They afford a stark and amoral insight into human behaviour in its full spectrum of virtues and frailties and glimpses of brilliant Chinese witticisms, too.

Origins of Zen
Translated by Koh Kok Kiang

Tsai in this book traces the origins and development of Zen in China with a light-hearted touch which is very much in keeping with the Zen spirit of absolute freedom and unbounded creativity.

Records of the Historian
Translated by Tang Nguok Kiong

Adapted from Records of the Historian, one of the greatest historical work China has produced, Tsai has illustrated the life and characteristics of the Four Lords of the Warring Strates.

Roots of Wisdom
Translated by Koh Kok Kiang

One of the gems of Chinese literature, whose advocacy of a steadfast nature and a life of simplicity, goodness, quiet joy and harmony with one's fellow beings and the world at large has great relevance in an age of rapid changes.

Sayings of Confucius
Translated by Goh Beng Choo

This book features the life of Confucius, selected sayings from The Analects and some of his more prominent pupils. It captures the warm relationship between the sage and his disciples, and offers food for thought for the modern readers.

Sayings of Han Fei Zi
Translated by Alan Chong

Tsai Chih Chung retold and interpreted the basic ideas of legalism, a classical political philosophy that advocates a draconian legal code, embodying a system of liberal reward and heavy penalty as the basis of government, in his unique style.

Sayings of Lao Zi
Translated by Koh Kok Kiang & Wong Lit Khiong

The thoughts of Lao Zi, the founder of Taoism, are presented here in a light-hearted manner. It features the selected sayings from Dao De Jing.

Sayings of Lao Zi Book 2
Translated by Koh Kok Kiang

In the second book, Tsai Chih Chung has tackled some of the more abstruse passages from the Dao De Jing which he has not included in the first volume of Sayings of Lao Zi.

Sayings of Lie Zi
Translated by Koh Kok Kiang

A famous Taoist sage whose sayings deals with universal themes such as the joy of living, reconciliation with death, the limitations of human knowledge, the role of chance events.

Sayings of Mencius
Translated by Mary Ng En Tzu

This book contains stories about the life of Mencius and various excerpts from "Mencius", one of the Four Books of the Confucian Classics, which contains the philosophy of Mencius.

Sayings of Zhuang Zi
Translated by Goh Beng Choo

Zhuang Zi's non-conformist and often humorous views of life have been creatively illustrated and simply presented by Tsai Chih Chung in this book.

Sayings of Zhuang Zi Book 2
Translated by Koh Kok Kiang

Zhuang Zi's book is valued for both its philosophical insights and as a work of great literary merit. Tsai's second book on Zhuang Zi shows maturity in his unique style.

Strange Tales of Liaozhai
Translated by Tang Nguok Kiong

In this book, Tsai Chih Chung has creatively illustrated 12 stories from the Strange Tales of Liaozhai, an outstanding Chinese classic written by Pu Songling in the early Qing Dynasty.

Zhong Yong
Translated by Mary Ng En Tzu

Zhong Yong, written by Zi Si, the grandson of Confucius, gives voice to the heart of the discipline of Confucius. Tsai has presented it in a most readable manner for the modern readers to explore with great delight.

Hilarious Chinese Classics by Tsai Chih Chung

Journey to the West 1

These books offer more than the all-too-familiar escapades of Tan Sanzang and his animal disciples. Under the creative pen of Tsai Chih Chung, *Journey to the West* still stays its course but takes a new route. En route from ancient China to India to acquire Buddhist scriptures, the Monk and his disciples veer off course frequently to dart into modern times to have fleeting exchanges with characters ranging from Ronald Reagan to Bunny Girls of the Playboy Club.

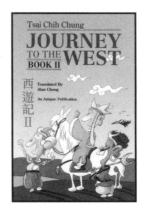

Journey to the West 2

Romance of the Three Kingdoms

Set in the turbulent Three Kingdoms Period, *Romance of the Three Kingdoms* relates the clever political manoeuvres and brilliant battle strategies used by the ambitious rulers as they fought one another for supremacy.

In this comic version, Tsai Chih Chung has illustrated in an entertaining way the four best-known episodes in the novel. Don't be surprised to see a warrior waving an Iraqi flag, a satellite dish fixed on top of an ancient Chinese building, and court officials playing mahjong or eating beef noodles, a favourite Taiwanese snack.

Latest Titles in Asiapac Comic Series

Battle Domestica

A satire about married life typified by a middle-aged couple who derive sadistic pleasure from mutual verbal assault.

Known as *Double Big Guns* in Taiwan, its Chinese edition has sold more than 400,000 copies worldwide.

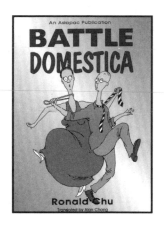

Sour Pack

There exist among us people who participate but are never committed; who are willing to give but attach more importance to what they get in return; who long for love but are terrified of being tied down.

Images of these people, their credo, and their lifestyles are reflected in the book. You may find in these cartoon characters familiar glimpses of yourself or those around you.

《亞太漫畫系列》

智謀叢畫

六韜

編著：王宣銘

翻譯：張家榮

亞太圖書有限公司出版